When We Were Very Young
and
Now We Are Six

When We Were Very Young
and
Now We Are Six

A. A. Milne
Illustrated by E. H. Shepard

EGMONT

We bring stories to life

When We Were Very Young, first published in 1924,
and *Now We Are Six*, first published in 1927
by Methuen & Co.Ltd.
Text by A. A. Milne and line illustrations by E. H. Shepard
copyright under the Berne Convention.

This edition published in Great Britain in 2005 by Dean,
an imprint of Egmont Books Limited,
239 Kensington High Street, London W8 6SA.

ISBN 0 603 56214 0

1 3 5 7 9 10 8 6 4 2

Printed and bound in Dubai

Contents

When We Were Very Young

"Vespers", being in the library of the Queen's Doll's House, is printed here by special permission.

CONTENTS

Now We Are Six

When We
Were Very Young

TO

Christopher Robin Milne

OR, AS HE PREFERS TO CALL HIMSELF,

BILLY MOON

THIS BOOK

WHICH OWES SO MUCH TO HIM

IS NOW

HUMBLY OFFERED

Just before we begin

At one time (but I have changed my mind now) I thought I was going to write a little Note at the top of each of these poems, in the manner of Mr William Wordsworth, who liked to tell his readers where he was staying, and which of his friends he was walking with, and what he was thinking about, when the idea of writing his poem came to him. You will find some lines about a swan here, if you get as far as that, and I should have explained to you in the Note that Christopher Robin, who feeds this swan in the mornings, has given him the name of "Pooh". This is a very fine name for a swan, because, if you call him and he doesn't come (which is a thing swans are good at), then you can pretend that you were just saying "Pooh!" to show how little you wanted him. Well, I should have told you that there are six cows who come down to Pooh's lake every afternoon to drink, and of course they say "Moo" as they come. So I thought to myself one fine day, walking with my friend Christopher Robin, "Moo rhymes with Pooh! Surely there is a bit of poetry to be got out of that?" Well, then, I began to think about the swan on his lake; and at first I thought how lucky it was that his name was Pooh; and then I didn't think about that any more . . . and the poem came quite differently from what I intended . . . and all I can say for it now is that, if it hadn't been for Christopher Robin, I shouldn't have written it; which, indeed, is all I can say for any of the others. So this is why these verses go about together, because they are all friends of Christopher Robin; and if I left out one because it was not quite like the one before, then I should have to leave out the one before because it was not quite like the next, which would be disappointing for them.

Then there is another thing. You may wonder sometimes who is supposed to be saying the verses. Is it the Author, that strange but uninteresting person, or is it Christopher Robin, or some other boy or girl, or Nurse, or Hoo? If I had followed Mr Wordsworth's plan, I could have explained this each time; as it is, you will have to decide for yourselves. If you are not quite sure, then it is probably Hoo. I don't know if you have ever met Hoo, but he is one of those curious children who look four on Monday, and eight on Tuesday, and are really twenty-eight on Saturday; and you never know whether it is the day when he can pronounce his "r's". He had a great deal to do with these verses. In fact, you might almost say that this book is entirely the unaided work of Christopher Robin, Hoo, and Mr Shepard, who drew the pictures. They have said "Thank you" politely to each other several times, and now they say it to you for taking them into your house. "Thank you so much for asking us. We've come."

A. A. M.

Corner-of-the-Street

Down by the corner of the street,
Where the three roads meet,
And the feet
Of the people as they pass go "Tweet-tweet-tweet",
Who comes tripping round the corner of the street?
One pair of shoes which are Nurse's;
One pair of slippers which are Percy's . . .
Tweet! Tweet! Tweet!

Buckingham Palace

They're changing guard at Buckingham Palace –
Christopher Robin went down with Alice.
Alice is marrying one of the guard.
"A soldier's life is terrible hard,"
                                   Says Alice.

They're changing guard at Buckingham Palace –
Christopher Robin went down with Alice.
We saw a guard in a sentry-box.
"One of the sergeants looks after their socks,"
                                   Says Alice.

They're changing guard at Buckingham Palace –
Christopher Robin went down with Alice.
We looked for the King, but he never came.
"Well, God take care of him, all the same,"
                                   Says Alice.

16

They're changing guard at Buckingham Palace –
Christopher Robin went down with Alice.
They've great big parties inside the grounds.
"I wouldn't be King for a hundred pounds,"
                              Says Alice.

They're changing guard at Buckingham Palace –
Christopher Robin went down with Alice.
A face looked out, but it wasn't the King's.
"He's much too busy a-signing things,"
                              Says Alice.

They're changing guard at Buckingham Palace –
Christopher Robin went down with Alice.
"Do you think the King knows all about *me*?"
"Sure to, dear, but it's time for tea,"
                              Says Alice.

Happiness

John had
Great Big
Waterproof
Boots on;
John had a
Great Big
Waterproof
Hat;

John had a
Great Big
Waterproof
Mackintosh –
And that
(Said John)
　Is
　That.

The Christening

What shall I call
  My dear little dormouse?
His eyes are small,
  But his tail is e-nor-mouse.

I sometimes call him Terrible John,
'Cos his tail goes on –
And on –
And on.
And I sometimes call him Terrible Jack,
'Cos his tail goes on to the end of his back.
And I sometimes call him Terrible James,
'Cos he says he likes me calling him names. . . .

  But I think I shall call him Jim,
  'Cos I *am* fond of him.

19

Puppy and I

I met a Man as I went walking;
We got talking,
Man and I.
"Where are you going to, Man?" I said
   (I said to the Man as he went by).
"Down to the village, to get some bread.
Will you come with me?" "No, not I."

I met a Horse as I went walking;
We got talking,
Horse and I.
"Where are you going to, Horse, today?"
   (I said to the Horse as he went by).
"Down to the village to get some hay.
Will you come with me?" "No, not I."

20

I met a Woman as I went walking;
We got talking,
Woman and I.
"Where are you going to, Woman, so early?"
  (I said to the Woman as she went by).
"Down to the village to get some barley.
Will you come with me?" "No, not I."

I met some Rabbits as I went walking;
We got talking,
Rabbits and I.
"Where are you going in your brown fur coats?"
  (I said to the Rabbits as they went by).
"Down to the village to get some oats.
Will you come with us?" "No, not I."

I met a Puppy as I went walking;
We got talking,
Puppy and I.
"Where are you going this nice fine day?"
   (I said to the Puppy as he went by).
"Up in the hills to roll and play."
"*I'll* come with you, Puppy," said I.

Twinkletoes

When the sun
Shines through the leaves of the apple-tree,
When the sun
Makes shadows of the leaves of the apple-tree,
Then I pass
On the grass
From one leaf to another
From one leaf to its brother
Tip-toe, tip-toe!
Here I go!

The Four Friends

Ernest was an elephant, a great big fellow,
  Leonard was a lion with a six-foot tail,
George was a goat, and his beard was yellow,
    And James was a very small snail.

Leonard had a stall, and a great big strong one,
  Ernest had a manger, and its walls were thick,
George found a pen, but I think it was the wrong one,
    And James sat down on a brick.

24

Ernest started trumpeting, and cracked his manger,
   Leonard started roaring, and shivered his stall,
James gave the huffle of a snail in danger
      And nobody heard him at all.

Ernest started trumpeting and raised such a rumpus,
   Leonard started roaring and trying to kick,
James went a journey with the goat's new compass
      And he reached the end of his brick.

25

Ernest was an elephant and very well-intentioned,
Leonard was a lion with a brave new tail,
George was a goat, as I think I have mentioned,
But James was only a snail.

Lines and Squares

Whenever I walk in a London street,
I'm ever so careful to watch my feet;
  And I keep in the squares,
  And the masses of bears,
Who wait at the corners all ready to eat
The sillies who tread on the lines of the street,
  Go back to their lairs,
  And I say to them, "Bears,
Just look how I'm walking in all the squares!"

27

And the little bears growl to each other, "He's mine,
As soon as he's silly and steps on a line."

And some of the bigger bears try to pretend
That they came round the corner to look for a friend;
And they try to pretend that nobody cares
Whether you walk on the lines or squares.
But only the sillies believe their talk;
It's ever so portant how you walk.

And it's ever so jolly to call out, "Bears,
Just watch me walking in all the squares!"

29

Brownie

In a corner of the bedroom is a great big curtain,
   Someone lives behind it, but I don't know who;
I think it is a Brownie, but I'm not quite certain.
   (Nanny isn't certain, too.)

I looked behind the curtain, but he went so quickly –
   Brownies never wait to say, "How do you do?"
They wriggle off at once because they're all so tickly.
   (Nanny says they're tickly too.)

Independence

I never did, I never did, I never *did* like
    "Now take care, dear!"
I never did, I never did, I never *did* want
    "Hold-my-hand";
I never did, I never did, I never *did* think much of
    "Not up there, dear!"
It's no good saying it. They don't understand.

Nursery Chairs

One of the chairs is South America,
One of the chairs is a ship at sea,
One is a cage for a great big lion,
And one is a chair for Me.

THE FIRST CHAIR
When I go up the Amazon,
I stop at night and fire a gun
  To call my faithful band.
And Indians in twos and threes,
Come silently between the trees,
  And wait for me to land.
And if I do not want to play
With any Indians today,
  I simply wave my hand.
And then they turn and go away –
They always understand.

32

THE SECOND CHAIR
I'm a great big lion in my cage,
   And I often frighten Nanny with a roar.
      Then I hold her very tight, and
        Tell her not to be so frightened –
   And she doesn't be so frightened any more.

33

The Third Chair

When I am in my ship, I see
  The other ships go sailing by.
A sailor leans and calls to me
  As his tall ship goes sailing by.
Across the sea he leans to me,
  Above the wind I hear him cry:
"Is this the way to Round-the-World?"
  He calls as he goes by.

34

THE FOURTH CHAIR

Whenever I sit in a high chair
For breakfast or dinner or tea,
I try to pretend that it's *my* chair,
And that I am a baby of three.

Shall I go off to South America?
Shall I put out in my ship to sea?
Or get in my cage and be lions and tigers?
Or – shall I be only Me?

Market Square

I had a penny,
A bright new penny,
I took my penny
   To the market square.
I wanted a rabbit,
A little brown rabbit,
And I looked for a rabbit
   'Most everywhere.

For I went to the stall where they sold sweet lavender
(*"Only a penny for a bunch of lavender!"*).
"Have you got a rabbit, 'cos I don't want lavender?"
   But they hadn't got a rabbit, not anywhere there.

I had a penny,
And I had another penny,
I took my pennies
  To the market square.
I did want a rabbit,
A little baby rabbit,
And I looked for rabbits
  'Most everywhere.

And I went to the stall where they sold fresh mackerel
("*Now then! Tuppence for a fresh-caught mackerel!*").
"Have you got a rabbit, 'cos I don't like mackerel?"
  But they hadn't got a rabbit, not anywhere there.

I found a sixpence,
A little white sixpence.
I took it in my hand
   To the market square.
I was buying my rabbit
(I do like rabbits),
And I looked for my rabbit
   'Most everywhere.

So I went to the stall where they sold fine saucepans
("*Walk up, walk up, sixpence for a saucepan!*").
"Could I have a rabbit, 'cos we've got two saucepans?"
   But they hadn't got a rabbit, not anywhere there.

42

I had nuffin',
No, I hadn't got nuffin',
So I didn't go down
    To the market square;
But I walked on the common
The old-gold common . . .
And I saw little rabbits
'Most everywhere!

So I'm sorry for the people who sell fine saucepans,
I'm sorry for the people who sell fresh mackerel,
I'm sorry for the people who sell sweet lavender,
    'Cos they haven't got a rabbit, not anywhere there!

Daffodowndilly

She wore her yellow sun-bonnet,
  She wore her greenest gown;
She turned to the south wind
  And curtsied up and down.
She turned to the sunlight
  And shook her yellow head,
And whispered to her neighbour:
  "Winter is dead."

Water-lilies

Where the water-lilies go
To and fro,
Rocking in the ripples of the water,
Lazy on a leaf lies the Lake King's daughter,
And the faint winds shake her.
Who will come and take her?
I will! I will!
Keep still! Keep still!
Sleeping on a leaf lies the Lake King's daughter . . .
Then the wind comes skipping
To the lilies on the water;
And the kind winds wake her.

Now who will take her?
With a laugh she is slipping
Through the lilies on the water.
Wait! Wait!
Too late, too late!
Only the water-lilies go
To and fro,
Dipping, dipping,
To the ripples of the water.

Disobedience

James James
Morrison Morrison
Weatherby George Dupree
Took great
Care of his Mother,
Though he was only three.
James James
Said to his Mother,
"Mother," he said, said he;
"You must never go down to the end of the town,
    if you don't go down with me."

James James
Morrison's Mother
Put on a golden gown,
James James
Morrison's Mother
Drove to the end of the town.

James James
Morrison's Mother
Said to herself, said she:
"I can get right down to the end of the town and
  be back in time for tea."

King John
  Put up a notice,
  "LOST or STOLEN or STRAYED!
  JAMES JAMES
  MORRISON'S MOTHER
  SEEMS TO HAVE BEEN MISLAID.
  LAST SEEN
  WANDERING VAGUELY:
  QUITE OF HER OWN ACCORD,
SHE TRIED TO GET DOWN TO THE END OF
    THE TOWN – **FORTY SHILLINGS REWARD!**"

48

James James
Morrison Morrison
(Commonly known as Jim)
Told his
Other relations
Not to go blaming *him*.
James James
Said to his Mother,
"Mother," he said, said he:
"You must *never* go down to the end of the town
without consulting me."

James James
Morrison's Mother
Hasn't been heard of since.
King John
Said he was sorry,
So did the Queen and Prince.
King John
(Somebody told me)
Said to a man he knew:
"If people go down to the end of the town, well, what
    can *anyone do?*"

(Now then, very softly)
J. J.
M. M.
W. G. Du P.
Took great
C/o his M*****
Though he was only 3.
J. J.
Said to his M*****
"M*****," he said, said he:

"You-must-never-go-down-to-the-end-of-the-town-if-
    you-don't-go-down-with ME!"

50

Spring Morning

Where am I going? I don't quite know.
Down to the stream where the king-cups grow –
Up to the hill where the pine-trees blow –
Anywhere, anywhere. *I* don't know.

Where am I going? The clouds sail by,
Little ones, baby ones, over the sky.
Where am I going? The shadows pass,
Little ones, baby ones, over the grass.

If you were a cloud, and sailed up there,
You'd sail on water as blue as air,
And you'd see me here in the fields and say:
"Doesn't the sky look green today?"

Where am I going? The high rooks call:
"It's awful fun to be born at all."
Where am I going? The ring-doves coo:
"We do have beautiful things to do."

If you were a bird, and lived on high,
You'd lean on the wind when the wind came by,
You'd say to the wind when it took you away:
"*That's* where I wanted to go today!"

Where am I going? I don't quite know.
What does it matter where people go?
Down to the wood where the blue-bells grow –
Anywhere, anywhere. *I* don't know.

The Island

If I had a ship,
I'd sail my ship,
I'd sail my ship
Through Eastern seas;
Down to a beach where the slow waves thunder –
The green curls over and the white falls under –
Boom! Boom! Boom!
On the sun-bright sand.
Then I'd leave my ship and I'd land,
And climb the steep white sand,

And climb to the trees,
The six dark trees,
The coco-nut trees on the cliff's green crown –
Hands and knees
To the coco-nut trees,
Face to the cliff as the stones patter down,
Up, up, up, staggering, stumbling,
Round the corner where the rock is crumbling,
Round this shoulder,
Over this boulder,
Up to the top where the six trees stand . . .

And there would I rest, and lie,
My chin in my hands, and gaze
At the dazzle of sand below,
And the green waves curling slow,
And the grey-blue distant haze
Where the sea goes up to the sky . . .

And I'd say to myself as I looked so lazily down at the
   sea:
"There's nobody else in the world, and the world was
   made for me."

The Three Foxes

Once upon a time there were three little foxes
Who didn't wear stockings, and they didn't wear sockses,
But they all had handkerchiefs to blow their noses,
And they kept their handkerchiefs in cardboard boxes.

They lived in the forest in three little houses,
And they didn't wear coats, and they didn't wear trousies,
They ran through the woods on their little bare tootsies,
And they played "Touch last" with a family of mouses.

They didn't go shopping in the High Street shopses,
But caught what they wanted in the woods and copses.
They all went fishing, and they caught three wormses,
They went out hunting, and they caught three wopses.

They went to a Fair, and they all won prizes –
Three plum-puddingses and three mince-pieses.
They rode on elephants and swang on swingses,
And hit three coco-nuts at coco-nut shieses.

That's all that I know of the three little foxes
Who kept their handkerchiefs in cardboard boxes.
They lived in the forest in three little houses,
But they didn't wear coats and they didn't wear trousies.
And they didn't wear stockings and they didn't wear sockses.

Politeness

If people ask me,
I always tell them:
"Quite well, thank you, I'm very glad to say."
If people ask me,
I always answer,
"Quite well, thank you, how are you today?"
I always answer,
I always tell them,
If they ask me
Politely . . .
BUT SOMETIMES

I wish

That they wouldn't.

Jonathan Jo

Jonathan Jo
Has a mouth like an "O"
And a wheelbarrow full of surprises;
If you ask for a bat,
Or for something like that,
He has got it, whatever the size is.

If you're wanting a ball,
It's no trouble at all;
Why, the more that you ask for, the merrier –
Like a hoop and a top,
And a watch that won't stop,
And some sweets, and an Aberdeen terrier.

Jonathan Jo
Has a mouth like an "O",
But this is what makes him so funny:
If you give him a smile,
Only once in a while,
Then he never expects any money!

At the Zoo

There are lions and roaring tigers, and enormous camels
    and things,
There are biffalo-buffalo-bisons, and a great big bear
    with wings,
There's a sort of a tiny potamus, and a tiny nosserus
    too –
But *I* gave buns to the elephant when *I* went down to
    the Zoo!

There are badgers and bidgers and bodgers, and a
    Super-in-tendent's House,
There are masses of goats, and a Polar, and different
    kinds of mouse,
And I think there's a sort of a something which is called
    a wallaboo –
But *I* gave buns to the elephant when *I* went down to
    the Zoo!

If you try to talk to the bison, he never quite understands;
You can't shake hands with a mingo – he doesn't like
    shaking hands.
And lions and roaring tigers *hate* saying, "How do you
    do?" –
But *I* give buns to the elephant when *I* go down to the
    Zoo!

Rice Pudding

What is the matter with Mary Jane?
She's crying with all her might and main,
And she won't eat her dinner – rice pudding again –
What *is* the matter with Mary Jane?

What is the matter with Mary Jane?
I've promised her dolls and a daisy-chain,
And a book about animals – all in vain –
What *is* the matter with Mary Jane?

What is the matter with Mary Jane?
She's perfectly well, and she hasn't a pain;
But, look at her, now she's beginning again! –
What *is* the matter with Mary Jane?

What is the matter with Mary Jane?
I've promised her sweets and a ride in the train,
And I've begged her to stop for a bit and explain –
What *is* the matter with Mary Jane?

What is the matter with Mary Jane?
She's perfectly well, and she hasn't a pain,
And it's lovely rice pudding for dinner again! –
What *is* the matter with Mary Jane?

Missing

Has anybody seen my mouse?

I opened his box for half a minute,
Just to make sure he was really in it,
And while I was looking, he jumped outside!
I tried to catch him, I tried, I tried . . .
I think he's somewhere about the house.
Has *anyone* seen my mouse?

Uncle John, have you seen my mouse?

Just a small sort of mouse, a dear little brown one,
He came from the country, he wasn't a town one,
So he'll feel all lonely in a London Street;
Why, what could he possibly find to eat?

He must be somewhere. I'll ask Aunt Rose:
Have *you* seen a mouse with a woffelly nose?
Oh, somewhere about –
He's just got out . . .

Hasn't *anybody* seen my mouse?

The King's Breakfast

The King asked
The Queen, and
The Queen asked
The Dairymaid:
"Could we have some butter for
The Royal slice of bread?"
The Queen asked
The Dairymaid,
The Dairymaid
Said, "Certainly,
I'll go and tell
The cow
Now
Before she goes to bed."

The Dairymaid
She curtsied,

And went and told
The Alderney:
"Don't forget the butter for
The Royal slice of bread."

The Alderney
Said sleepily:
"You'd better tell
His Majesty

That many people nowadays
Like marmalade
Instead."

The Dairymaid
Said, "Fancy!"
And went to
Her Majesty.
She curtsied to the Queen, and
She turned a little red:
"Excuse me,
Your Majesty,
For taking of
The liberty,
But marmalade is tasty, if
It's very
Thickly
Spread."

The Queen said,
"Oh!"
And went to
His Majesty:
"Talking of the butter for
The Royal slice of bread,

74

Many people
Think that
Marmalade
Is nicer.
Would you like to try a little
Marmalade
Instead?"

The King said,
"Bother!"
And then he said,
"Oh, deary me!"
The King sobbed, "Oh, deary me!"
And went back to bed.
"Nobody,"
He whimpered,
"Could call me
A fussy man;
I *only* want
A little bit
Of butter for
My bread!"

The Queen said,
"There, there!"
And went to
The Dairymaid.

The Dairymaid
Said, "There, there!"
And went to the shed.

The cow said,
"There, there!
I didn't really
Mean it;
Here's milk for his porringer
And butter for his bread."

The Queen took
The butter

And brought it to
His Majesty;
The King said,
"Butter, eh?"
And bounced out of bed.
"Nobody," he said,
As he kissed her
Tenderly,
"Nobody," he said,
As he slid down
The banisters,
"Nobody,
My darling,
Could call me
A fussy man –
BUT
I do like a little bit of butter to my bread!"

Hoppity

Christopher Robin goes
Hoppity, hoppity,

Hoppity, hoppity, hop.
Whenever I tell him
Politely to stop it, he
Says he can't possibly stop.

If he stopped hopping, he couldn't go anywhere,
Poor little Christopher
Couldn't go anywhere . . .
That's why he *always* goes
Hoppity, hoppity,
Hoppity,
Hoppity,
Hop.

At Home

I want a soldier
(A soldier in a busby),
I want a soldier to come and play with me.
I'd give him cream-cakes
(Big ones, sugar ones),
I'd give him cream-cakes and cream for his tea.

I want a soldier
(A tall one, a red one),
I want a soldier who plays on the drum.
Daddy's going to get one
(He's written to the shopman),
Daddy's going to get one as soon as he can come.

80

The Wrong House

I went into a house, and it wasn't a house,
  It has big steps and a great big hall;
But it hasn't got a garden,
      A garden,
      A garden,
  It isn't like a house at all.

I went into a house, and it wasn't a house,
  It has a big garden and great high wall;
But it hasn't got a may-tree,
      A may-tree,
      A may-tree,
  It isn't like a house at all.

I went into a house and it wasn't a house –
  Slow white petals from the may-tree fall;
But it hasn't got a blackbird,
        A blackbird,
        A blackbird,
  It isn't like a house at all.

I went into a house, and I thought it was a house,
  I could hear from the may-tree the blackbird call . . .
But nobody listened to it,
        Nobody
        Liked it,
  Nobody wanted it at all.

Summer Afternoon

Six brown cows walk down to drink
   (All the little fishes blew bubbles at the may-fly).
Splash goes the first as he comes to the brink,
   Swish go the tails of the five who follow . . .
Twelve brown cows bend drinking there
   (All the little fishes went waggle-tail, waggle-tail) –
Six from the water and six from the air;
Up and down the river darts a blue-black swallow.

The Dormouse and the Doctor

There once was a Dormouse who lived in a bed
Of delphiniums (blue) and geraniums (red),
And all the day long he'd a wonderful view
Of geraniums (red) and delphiniums (blue).

A Doctor came hurrying round, and he said:
"Tut-tut, I am sorry to find you in bed.

84

Just say 'Ninety-Nine', while I look at your chest . . .
Don't you find that chrysanthemums answer the best?"

The Dormouse looked round at the view and replied
(When he'd said "Ninety-nine") that he'd tried and
    he'd tried,
And much the most answering things that he knew
Were geraniums (red) and delphiniums (blue).

The Doctor stood frowning and shaking his head,
And he took up his shiny silk hat as he said:
"What the patient requires is a change," and he went
To see some chrysanthemum people in Kent.

The Dormouse lay there, and he gazed at the view
Of geraniums (red) and delphiniums (blue),
And he knew there was nothing he wanted instead
Of delphiniums (blue) and geraniums (red).

The Doctor came back and, to show what he meant,
He had brought some chrysanthemum cuttings from Kent.

"Now *these*," he remarked, "give a *much* better view
Than geraniums (red) and delphiniums (blue)."

They took out their spades and they dug up the bed
Of delphiniums (blue) and geraniums (red),

And they planted chrysanthemums (yellow and white).
"And *now*," said the Doctor, "we'll *soon* have you right."

The Dormouse looked out, and he said with a sigh:
"I suppose all these people know better than I.
It was silly, perhaps, but I *did* like the view
Of geraniums (red) and delphiniums (blue)."

The Doctor came round and examined his chest,
And ordered him Nourishment, Tonics, and Rest.
"How very effective," he said, as he shook
The thermometer, "all these chrysanthemums look!"

The Dormouse turned over to shut out the sight
Of the endless chrysanthemums (yellow and white).
"How lovely," he thought, "to be back in a bed
Of delphiniums (blue) and geraniums (red)."

The Doctor said, "Tut! It's another attack!"
And ordered him Milk and Massage-of-the-back,
And Freedom-from-worry and Drives-in-a-car,
And murmured, "How sweet your chrysanthemums are!"

The Dormouse lay there with his paws to his eyes,
And imagined himself such a pleasant surprise:
"I'll *pretend* the chrysanthemums turn to a bed
Of delphiniums (blue) and geraniums (red)!"

The Doctor next morning was rubbing his hands,
And saying, "There's nobody quite understands
These cases as I do! The cure has begun!
How fresh the chrysanthemums look in the sun!"

The Dormouse lay happy, his eyes were so tight
He could see no chrysanthemums, yellow or white.
And all that he felt at the back of his head
Were delphiniums (blue) and geraniums (red).

And that is the reason (Aunt Emily said)
If a Dormouse gets in a chrysanthemum bed,
You will find (so Aunt Emily says) that he lies
Fast asleep on his front with his paws to his eyes.

Shoes and Stockings

There's a cavern in the mountain where the old men meet
(Hammer, hammer, hammer . . .
Hammer, hammer, hammer . . .)
They make gold slippers for my lady's feet
(Hammer, hammer, hammer . . .
Hammer, hammer, hammer . . .)
My lady is marrying her own true knight,
White her gown, and her veil is white,
But she must have slippers on her dainty feet.
Hammer, hammer, hammer . . .
Hammer.

There's a cottage by the river where the old wives meet
(Chatter, chatter, chatter . . .
Chatter, chatter, chatter . . .)
They weave gold stockings for my lady's feet

(Chatter, chatter, chatter . . .
Chatter, chatter, chatter . . .).
My lady is going to her own true man,
Youth to youth, since the world began,
But she must have stockings on her dainty feet.
Chatter, chatter, chatter . . .
Chatter.

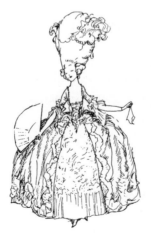

Sand-between-the-toes

I went down to the shouting sea,
Taking Christopher down with me,
For Nurse had given us sixpence each –
And down we went to the beach.

We had sand in the eyes and the ears and the nose,
And sand in the hair, and sand-between-the-toes.
Whenever a good nor'-wester blows,
Christopher is certain of
Sand-between-the-toes.

The sea was galloping grey and white;
Christopher clutched his sixpence tight;
We clambered over the humping sand –
And Christopher held my hand.

We had sand in the eyes and the ears and the nose,
And sand in the hair, and sand-between-the-toes.
Whenever a good nor'-wester blows,
Christopher is certain of
Sand-between-the-toes.

There was a roaring in the sky;
The sea-gulls cried as they blew by,
We tried to talk, but had to shout –
Nobody else was out.

When we got home, we had sand in the hair,
In the eyes and the ears and everywhere;
Whenever a good nor'-wester blows,
Christopher is found with
Sand-between-the-toes.

Knights and Ladies

There is in my old picture book
A page at which I like to look,
Where knights and squires come riding down
The cobbles of some steep old town,
And ladies from beneath the eaves
Flutter their bravest handkerchiefs,
Or, smiling proudly, toss down gages . . .
But that was in the Middle Ages.
It wouldn't happen now; but still,
Whenever I look up the hill
Where, dark against the green and blue,
The firs come marching, two by two,
I wonder if perhaps I *might*

See suddenly a shining knight
Winding his way from blue to green –
Exactly as it would have been
Those many, many years ago . . .

Perhaps I might. You never know.

Little Bo-Peep and Little Boy Blue

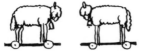

"What have you done with your sheep,
    Little Bo-Peep?
What have you done with your sheep,
    Bo-Peep?"
"Little Boy Blue, what fun!
I've lost them, every one!"
"Oh, what a thing to have done,
    Little Bo-Peep!"

"What have you done with your sheep,
    Little Boy Blue?
What have you done with your sheep,
    Boy Blue?"
"Little Bo-Peep, my sheep
Went off, when I was asleep."
"I'm sorry about your sheep,
    Little Boy Blue."

"What are you going to do,
          Little Bo-Peep?
What are you going to do,
          Bo-Peep?"
"Little Boy Blue, you'll see
They'll all come home to tea."
"They wouldn't do that for me,
          Little Bo-Peep."

"What are you going to do,
          Little Boy Blue?
What are you going to do,
          Boy Blue?"
"Little Bo-Peep, I'll blow
My horn for an hour or so."
"Isn't that rather slow,
          Little Boy Blue?"

"Whom are you going to marry,
  Little Bo-Peep?
Whom are you going to marry,
  Bo-Peep?"
"Little Boy Blue, Boy Blue,
I'd like to marry you."
"I think I should like it too,
  Little Bo-Peep."

"Where are we going to live,
  Little Boy Blue?
Where are we going to live,
  Boy Blue?"

"Little Bo-Peep, Bo-Peep,
Up in the hills with the sheep."
"And you'll love your little Bo-Peep,
Little Boy Blue?"

"I'll love you for ever and ever,
Little Bo-Peep.
I'll love you for ever and ever,
Bo-Peep."
"Little Boy Blue, my dear,
Keep near, keep very near."
"I shall be always here,
Little Bo-Peep."

100

The Mirror

Between the woods the afternoon
Is fallen in a golden swoon.
The sun looks down from quiet skies
To where a quiet water lies,
   And silent trees stoop down to trees.
And there I saw a white swan make
Another white swan in the lake;
And, breast to breast, both motionless,
They waited for the wind's caress . . .
   And all the water was at ease.

Halfway Down

Halfway down the stairs
Is a stair
Where I sit.
There isn't any
Other stair
Quite like
It.
I'm not at the bottom,
I'm not at the top;
So this is the stair
Where
I always
Stop.

Halfway up the stairs
Isn't up,
And isn't down.
It isn't in the nursery,
It isn't in the town.
And all sorts of funny thoughts
Run round my head:
"It isn't really
Anywhere!
It's somewhere else
Instead!"

The Invaders

In careless patches through the wood
The clumps of yellow primrose stood,
And sheets of white anemones,
Like driven snow against the trees,
Had covered up the violet,
But left the blue-bell bluer yet.

Along the narrow carpet ride,
With primroses on either side,
Between their shadows and the sun,
The cows came slowly, one by one,
Breathing the early morning air
And leaving it still sweeter there.
And, one by one, intent upon
Their purposes, they followed on
In ordered silence . . . and were gone.

But all the little wood was still,
As if it waited so, until
Some blackbird on an outpost yew,
Watching the slow procession through,
Lifted his yellow beak at last
To whistle that the line had passed . . .
Then all the wood began to sing
Its morning anthem to the spring.

Before Tea

Emmeline
Has not been seen
For more than a week. She slipped between
The two tall trees at the end of the green . . .
We all went after her. "*Emmeline!*"

"Emmeline,
I didn't mean –
I only said that your hands weren't clean."
We went to the trees at the end of the green . . .
But Emmeline
Was not to be seen.

Emmeline
Came slipping between
The two tall trees at the end of the green.
We all ran up to her. "Emmeline!
Where have you been?
Where have you been?
Why, it's more than a week!" And Emmeline
Said, "Sillies, I went and saw the Queen.
She says my hands are *purfickly* clean!"

Teddy Bear

A bear, however hard he tries,
Grows tubby without exercise.
Our Teddy Bear is short and fat,
Which is not to be wondered at;
He gets what exercise he can
By falling off the ottoman,
But generally seems to lack
The energy to clamber back.

Now tubbiness is just the thing
Which gets a fellow wondering;
And Teddy worried lots about
The fact that he was rather stout.

108

He thought: "If only I were thin!
But how does anyone begin?"
He thought: "It really isn't fair
To grudge me exercise and air."

For many weeks he pressed in vain
His nose against the window-pane,
And envied those who walked about
Reducing their unwanted stout.
None of the people he could see
"Is quite" (he said) "as fat as me!"
Then, with a still more moving sigh,
"I mean" (he said) "as fat as I!"

Now Teddy, as was only right,
Slept in the ottoman at night,
And with him crowded in as well
More animals than I can tell;
Not only these, but books and things,
Such as a kind relation brings –
Old tales of "Once upon a time,"
And history retold in rhyme.

One night it happened that he took
A peep at an old picture book,
Wherein he came across by chance
The picture of a King of France

(A stoutish man) and, down below,
These words: "King Louis So and So,
Nicknamed 'The Handsome'!" There he sat,
And *(think of it!) the man was fat!*

Our bear rejoiced like anything
To read about this famous King,
Nicknamed "The Handsome". There he sat,
And certainly the man was fat.
Nicknamed "The Handsome". Not a doubt
The man was definitely stout.
Why then, a bear (for all his tub)
Might yet be named "The Handsome Cub"!

"Might yet be named." Or did he mean
That years ago he "might have been"?
For now he felt a slight misgiving:
"Is Louis So and So still living?
Fashions in beauty have a way
Of altering from day to day.
Is 'Handsome Louis' with us yet?
Unfortunately I forget."

Next morning (nose to window-pane)
The doubt occurred to him again.
One question hammered in his head:
"Is he alive or is he dead?"
Thus, nose to pane, he pondered; but
The lattice window, loosely shut,
Swung open. With one startled "Oh!"
Our Teddy disappeared below.

There happened to be passing by
A plump man with a twinkling eye,
Who, seeing Teddy in the street,
Raised him politely to his feet,

And murmured kindly in his ear
Soft words of comfort and of cheer:
"Well, well!" "Allow me!" "Not at all."
"Tut-tut! A very nasty fall."

Our Teddy answered not a word;
It's doubtful if he even heard.
Our bear could only look and look:
The stout man in the picture book!
That "handsome" King – could this be he,
This man of adiposity?
"Impossible," he thought. "But still,
No harm in asking. Yes I will!"

"Are you," he said, "by any chance
His Majesty the King of France?"
The other answered, "I am that,"
Bowed stiffly, and removed his hat;
Then said, "Excuse me," with an air,
"But is it Mr Edward Bear?"
And Teddy, bending very low,
Replied politely, "Even so!"

They stood beneath the window there,
The King and Mr Edward Bear,
And, handsome, if a trifle fat,
Talked carelessly of this and that . . .

114

Then said His Majesty, "Well, well,
I must get on," and rang the bell.
"Your bear, I think," he smiled. "Good-day!"
And turned, and went upon his way.

A bear, however hard he tries,
Grows tubby without exercise.
Our Teddy Bear is short and fat,
Which is not to be wondered at.
But do you think it worries him
To know that he is far from slim?
No, just the other way about –
He's *proud* of being short and stout.

Bad Sir Brian Botany

Sir Brian had a battleaxe with great big knobs on;
    He went among the villagers and blipped them on
    the head.
On Wednesday and on Saturday, but mostly on the
    latter day,
    He called at all the cottages, and this is what he said:

    "I am Sir Brian!" *(ting-ling)*
    "I am Sir Brian!" *(rat-tat)*
    "I am Sir Brian, as bold as a lion –
    Take *that!* – and *that!* – and *that!*"

Sir Brian had a pair of boots with great big spurs on,
    A fighting pair of which he was particularly fond.
On Tuesday and on Friday, just to make the street look
    tidy,
    He'd collect the passing villagers and kick them in
    the pond.

116

"I am Sir Brian!" (*sper-lash!*)
"I am Sir Brian!" (*sper-losh!*)
"I am Sir Brian, as bold as a lion –
Is anyone else for a wash?"

Sir Brian woke one morning, and he couldn't find his
    battleaxe;
  He walked into the village in his second pair of
    boots.
He had gone a hundred paces, when the street was full
    of faces,
  And the villagers were round him with ironical
    salutes.

117

"You are Sir Brian? Indeed!
You are Sir Brian? Dear, dear!
You are Sir Brian, as bold as a lion?
Delighted to meet you here!"

Sir Brian went a journey, and he found a lot of duck-weed:

They pulled him out and dried him, and they blipped
him on the head.
They took him by the breeches, and they hurled him
into ditches,
And they pushed him under waterfalls, and this is
what they said:

118

"You are Sir Brian – don't laugh,
  You are Sir Brian – don't cry;
You are Sir Brian, as bold as a lion –
  Sir Brian, the lion, good-bye!"

Sir Brian struggled home again, and chopped up his
  battleaxe,
  Sir Brian took his fighting boots, and threw them in
    the fire.
He is quite a different person now he hasn't got his
  spurs on,
  And he goes about the village as B. Botany, Esquire.

"I am Sir Brian? Oh, *no!*
  I am Sir Brian? Who's he?
I haven't got any title, I'm Botany –
  Plain Mr Botany (B)."

119

In the Fashion

A lion has a tail and a very fine tail,
And so has an elephant, and so has a whale,
And so has a crocodile, and so has a quail –
    They've all got tails but me.

If I had sixpence I would buy one;
I'd say to the shopman, "Let me try one";
I'd say to the elephant, "This is *my* one."
    They'd all come round to see.

Then I'd say to the lion, "Why, *you've* got a tail!
And so has the elephant, and so has the whale!
And, look! There's a crocodile! *He's* got a tail!
    You've all got tails like me!"

120

The Alchemist

There lives an old man at the top of the street,
And the end of his beard reaches down to his feet,
And he's just the one person I'm longing to meet,
    I think that he sounds so exciting;
For he talks all the day to his tortoiseshell cat,
And he asks about this, and explains about that,
And at night he puts on a big wide-awake* hat
    And sits in the writing-room, writing.

*So as not to go to sleep.

121

He has worked all his life (and he's terribly old)
At a wonderful spell which says, "Lo and behold!
Your nursery fender is gold!" – and it's gold!
    (Or the tongs, or the rod for the curtain);
But somehow he hasn't got hold of it quite,
Or the liquid you pour on it first isn't right,
So that's why he works at it night after night
    Till he knows he can do it for certain.

Growing Up

I've got shoes with grown-up laces,
I've got knickers and a pair of braces,
I'm all ready to run some races.
    Who's coming out with me?

I've got a nice new pair of braces,
I've got shoes with new brown laces,
I know wonderful paddly places.
    Who's coming out with me?

Every morning my new grace is,
"Thank you, God, for my nice braces;
I can tie my new brown laces."
    Who's coming out with me?

If I were King

I often wish I were a King,
And then I could do anything.

If only I were King of Spain,
I'd take my hat off in the rain.

If only I were King of France,
I wouldn't brush my hair for aunts.

I think, if I were King of Greece,
I'd push things off the mantelpiece.

If I were King of Norroway,
I'd ask an elephant to stay.

If I were King of Babylon,
I'd leave my button gloves undone.

If I were King of Timbuctoo,
I'd think of lovely things to do.

If I were King of anything,
I'd tell the soldiers, "I'm the King!"

Vespers

Little Boy kneels at the foot of the bed,
Droops on the little hands little gold head.
Hush! Hush! Whisper who dares!
Christopher Robin is saying his prayers.

God bless Mummy. I know that's right.
Wasn't it fun in the bath tonight?
The cold's so cold, and the hot's so hot.
Oh! *God bless Daddy* – I quite forgot.

If I open my fingers a little bit more,
I can see Nanny's dressing-gown on the door.
It's a beautiful blue, but it hasn't a hood.
Oh! *God bless Nanny and make her good.*

Mine has a hood, and I lie in bed,
And pull the hood right over my head,
And I shut my eyes, and I curl up small,
And nobody knows that I'm there at all.

Oh! *Thank you, God, for a lovely day.*
And what was the other I had to say?
I said "Bless Daddy," so what can it be?
Oh! Now I remember it. *God bless Me.*

Little Boy kneels at the foot of the bed,
Droops on the little hands little gold head.
Hush! Hush! Whisper who dares!
Christopher Robin is saying his prayers.

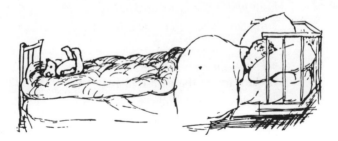

126

Now We Are Six

TO

Anne Darlington

NOW SHE IS SEVEN
AND
BECAUSE SHE IS
SO
SPESHAL

Introduction

When you are reciting poetry, which is a thing we never do, you find sometimes, just as you are beginning, that Uncle John is still telling Aunt Rose that if he can't find his spectacles he won't be able to hear properly, and does she know where they are; and by the time everybody has stopped looking for them, you are at the last verse, and in another minute they will be saying, "Thank-you, thank-you," without really knowing what it was all about. So, next time, you are more careful; and, just before you begin you say, "Er-h'r'm!" very loudly, which means, "Now then, here we are"; and everybody stops talking and looks at you; which is what you want. So then you get in the way of saying it whenever you are asked to recite . . . and sometimes it is just as well, and sometimes it isn't . . . and by and by you find yourself saying it without thinking. Well, this bit which I am writing, called Introduction, is really the er-h'r'm of the book, and I have put it in, partly so as not to take you by surprise, and partly because I can't do without it now. There are some very clever writers who say that it is quite easy not to have an er-h'r'm, but I don't agree with them. I think it is much easier not to have all the rest of the book.

What I want to explain in the Introduction is this. We have been nearly three years writing this book. We began it when we were very young . . . and now we are six. So, of course, bits of it seem rather babyish to us, almost as if they had slipped out of some other book by mistake. On page whatever-it-is there is a thing which is simply three-ish, and when we read it to ourselves just now we said, "Well, well, well," and turned over rather quickly. So we want you to know that the name of the book doesn't mean that this is us being six all the time, but that it is about as far as we've got at present, and we half think of stopping there.

A. A. M.

P. S. – Pooh wants us to say that he thought it was a different book; and he hopes you won't mind, but he walked through it one day, looking for his friend Piglet, and sat down on some of the pages by mistake.

Solitude

I have a house where I go
   When there's too many people,
I have a house where I go
   Where no one can be;
I have a house where I go,
Where nobody ever says "No"
Where no one says anything – so
   There is no one but me.

King John's Christmas

King John was not a good man –
   He had his little ways.
And sometimes no one spoke to him
   For days and days and days.
And men who came across him,
   When walking in the town,
Gave him a supercilious stare,
   Or passed with noses in the air –
And bad King John stood dumbly there,
   Blushing beneath his crown.

King John was not a good man,
   And no good friends had he.
He stayed in every afternoon . . .
   But no one came to tea.
And, round about December,

The cards upon his shelf
Which wished him lots of Christmas cheer,
And fortune in the coming year,
Were never from his near and dear,
But only from himself.

King John was not a good man,
  Yet had his hopes and fears.
They'd given him no present now
  For years and years and years.
But every year at Christmas,
  While minstrels stood about,
Collecting tribute from the young
For all the songs they might have sung,
He stole away upstairs and hung
  A hopeful stocking out.

King John was not a good man,
  He lived his life aloof;
Alone he thought a message out
  While climbing up the roof.
He wrote it down and propped it
  Against the chimney stack:
"TO ALL AND SUNDRY – NEAR AND FAR –
F. CHRISTMAS IN PARTICULAR."
And signed it not "Johannes R."
  But very humbly, "JACK."

"I want some crackers,
  And I want some candy;
I think a box of chocolates
  Would come in handy;
I don't mind oranges,

136

I do like nuts!
And I SHOULD like a pocket-knife
    That really cuts.
And, oh! Father Christmas, if you love me at all,
Bring me a big, red india-rubber ball!"

King John was not a good man –
    He wrote this message out,
And gat him to his room again,
    Descending by the spout.
And all that night he lay there,
    A prey to hopes and fears.
"I think that's him a-coming now,"
(Anxiety bedewed his brow.)
"He'll bring one present, anyhow –
    The first I've had for years."

"Forget about the crackers,
    And forget about the candy;
I'm sure a box of chocolates
    Would never come in handy;
I don't like oranges,
    I don't want nuts,
And I HAVE got a pocket-knife
    That almost cuts.
But oh! Father Christmas, if you love me at all,
Bring me a big, red india-rubber ball!"

King John was not a good man –
    Next morning when the sun
Rose up to tell a waiting world
    That Christmas had begun,
And people seized their stockings,
    And opened them with glee,
And crackers, toys and games appeared,
And lips with sticky sweets were smeared,
King John said grimly: "As I feared,
    Nothing again for me!"

"I did want crackers,
    And I did want candy;
I know a box of chocolates
    Would come in handy;
I do love oranges,
    I did want nuts.
I haven't got a pocket-knife –
    Not one that cuts.
And, oh! if Father Christmas had loved me at all,
He would have brought a big, red india-rubber ball!"

138

King John stood by the window,
    And frowned to see below
The happy bands of boys and girls
    All playing in the snow.
A while he stood there watching,
    And envying them all . . .
When through the window big and red
There hurtled by his royal head,
And bounced and fell upon the bed,
    An india-rubber ball!

AND OH, FATHER CHRISTMAS
    MY BLESSINGS ON YOU FALL
        FOR BRINGING HIM
        A BIG, RED
        INDIA-RUBBER
        BALL!

139

Busy

I think I am a Muffin Man. I haven't got a bell,
I haven't got the muffin things that muffin people sell.

Perhaps I am a postman. No, I think I am a Tram.
I'm feeling rather funny and I don't know *what* I am –

BUT
Round about
And *round* about
And *round* about I go –
All around the table,
The table in the nursery –

Round about
And round about
And round about I go:
I think I am a Traveller escaping from a Bear;

I think I am an Elephant,
Behind another Elephant
Behind another Elephant who isn't really there . . .

141

SO
Round about
And *round* about
And *round* about and *round* about
And *round* about
And *round* about
   I go.

I think I am a Ticket Man who's selling tickets – please,

I think I am a Doctor who is visiting a Sneeze;

142

Perhaps I'm just a Nanny who is walking with a pram
I'm feeling rather funny and I don't know *what* I am –

BUT
Round about
And *round* about
And *round* about I go –
All round the table,
The table in the nursery –
Round about
And *round* about
And *round* about I go.

I think I am a Puppy, so I'm hanging out my tongue;

I think I am Camel who
Is looking for a Camel who
Is looking for a Camel who is looking for its Young . . .

SO
Round about
And *round* about
And *round* about and *round* about
And *round* about
And *round* about
I go.

Sneezles

Christopher Robin
Had wheezles
And sneezles,
They bundled him
Into
His bed.
They gave him what goes
With a cold in the nose,
And some more for a cold
In the head.
They wondered
If wheezles
Could turn
Into measles,
If sneezles
Would turn
Into mumps;

145

They examined his chest
For a rash,
And the rest
Of his body for swellings and lumps.
They sent for some doctors
In sneezles
And wheezles
To tell them what ought
To be done.

All sorts and conditions
Of famous physicians
Came hurrying round
At a run.
They all made a note
Of the state of his throat,
They asked if he suffered from thirst;

146

They asked if the sneezles
Came *after* the wheezles,
Or if the first sneezle
Came first.
They said, "If you teazle
A sneezle
Or wheezle,
A measle
May easily grow.
But humour or pleazle
The wheezle
Or sneezle,
The measle
Will certainly go."

They expounded the reazles
For sneezles
And wheezles,
The manner of measles
When new.
They said "If he freezles
In draughts and in breezles,
Then PHTHEEZLES
May even ensue"

Christopher Robin
Got up in the morning,
The sneezles had vanished away.

And the look in his eye
Seemed to say to the sky,
"Now, how to amuse them today?"

Binker

Binker – what I call him – is a secret of my own,
And Binker is the reason why I never feel alone.
Playing in the nursery, sitting on the stair,
Whatever I am busy at, Binker will be there.

    Oh, Daddy is clever, he's a clever sort of man,
    And Mummy is the best since the world began,
    And Nanny is Nanny, and I call her Nan –
              But they can't
              See
              Binker.

Binker's always talking, 'cos I'm teaching him to speak:
He sometimes likes to do it in a funny sort of squeak,

149

And he sometimes likes to do it in a hoodling sort of roar . . .
And I have to do it for him 'cos his throat is rather sore.

Oh, Daddy is clever, he's a clever sort of man,
And Mummy knows all that anybody can.
And Nanny is Nanny, and I call her Nan –
But they don't
Know
Binker.

Binker's brave as lions when we're running in the park;
Binker's brave as tigers when we're lying in the dark;
Binker's brave as elephants. He never, never cries . . .
Except (like other people) when the soap gets in his eyes.

Oh, Daddy is Daddy, he's a Daddy sort of man,
And Mummy is as Mummy as anybody can,
And Nanny is Nanny, and I call her Nan . . .
      But they're not
      Like
      Binker.

Binker isn't greedy, but he does like things to eat,
So I have to say to people when they're giving me
   a sweet,
"Oh, Binker wants a chocolate, so could you give
   me two?"
And then I eat is for him, 'cos his teeth are rather
   new.

Well, I'm very fond of Daddy, but he hasn't time to
  play,
And I'm very fond of Mummy, but she sometimes
  goes away,
And I'm often cross with Nanny when she wants to
  brush my hair . . .

But Binker's always Binker, and is certain to be there.

Cherry Stones

Tinker, Tailor,

Soldier, Sailor,

Rich Man, Poor Man,

Ploughboy, Thief –

And what about a Cowboy,
Policeman, Jailer,
Engine-driver,
Or Pirate Chief?
What about a Postman – or a Keeper at the Zoo?
What about the Circus Man who lets the people
    through?
And the man who takes the pennies for the round-
    abouts and swings?
Or the man who plays the organ, and the other man
    who sings?
What about a Conjuror with rabbits in his pockets?
What about a Rocket Man who's always making
    rockets?

154

Oh, there's such a lot of things to do and such a lot to be
That there's always lots of cherries on my little cherry tree!

The Knight Whose Armour Didn't Squeak

Of all the Knights in Appledore
    The wisest was Sir Thomas Tom.
He multiplied as far as four,
    And knew what nine was taken from
To make eleven. He could write
A letter to another Knight.

156

No other Knight in all the land
  Could do the things which he could do.
Not only did he understand
  The way to polish swords, but knew
What remedy a Knight should seek
Whose armour had begun to squeak.

And, if he didn't fight too much,
  It wasn't that he did not care
For blips and buffetings and such,
  But felt that it was hardly fair
To risk, by frequent injuries,
A brain as delicate as his.

His castle (Castle Tom) was set
  Conveniently on a hill;
And daily, when it wasn't wet,
  He paced the battlements until
Some smaller Knight who couldn't swim
Should reach the moat and challenge him.

157

Or sometimes, feeling full of fight,
  He hurried out to scour the plain,
And, seeing some approaching Knight,
  He either hurried home again,
Or hid; and, when the foe was past,
Blew a triumphant trumpet-blast.

One day when good Sir Thomas Tom
  Was resting in a handy ditch,
The noises he was hiding from,
  Though very much the noises which
He'd always hidden from before,
Seemed somehow less . . . Or was it more?

The trotting horse, the trumpet's blast,
  The whistling sword, the armour's squeak,
These, and especially the last,
  Had clattered by him all the week.
Was this the same, or was it not?
Something was different. But what?

159

Sir Thomas raised a cautious ear
  And listened as Sir Hugh went by,
And suddenly he seemed to hear
  (Or not to hear) the reason why
This stranger made a nicer sound
Than other Knights who lived around.

Sir Thomas watched the way he went –
  His rage was such he couldn't speak,
For years they'd called him down in Kent
  The Knight Whose Armour Didn't Squeak!
Yet here and now he looked upon
Another Knight whose squeak had gone.

160

He rushed to where his horse was tied;
    He spurred it to a rapid trot.
The only fear he felt inside
    About his enemy was not
"How sharp his sword?" "How stout his heart?"
But "Has he got too long a start?"

Sir Hugh was singing, hand on hip,
    When something sudden came along,
And caught him a terrific blip
    Right in the middle of his song.

"A thunderstorm!" he thought "Of course!"
And toppled gently off his horse.

Then said the good Sir Thomas Tom,
 Dismounting with a friendly air,
"Allow me to extract you from
 The heavy armour that you wear.
At times like these the bravest Knight
May find his armour much too tight."

A hundred yards or so beyond
 The scene of brave Sir Hugh's defeat
Sir Thomas found a useful pond,
 And, careful not to wet his feet,
He brought the armour to the brink
And flung it in . . . and watched it sink.

So ever after, more and more,
  The men of Kent would proudly speak
Of Thomas Tom of Appledore,
  "The Knight Whose Armour Didn't Squeak."
Whilst Hugh, the Knight who gave him best,
Squeaks just as badly as the rest.

163

Buttercup Days

Where is Anne?
   Head above the buttercups,
Walking by the stream,
   Down among the buttercups.
Where is Anne?
Walking with her man,
Lost in a dream,
   Lost among the buttercups.
What has she got in that little brown head?
Wonderful thoughts which can never be said.
What has she got in that firm little fist of hers?
Somebody's thumb, and it feels like Christopher's.
   Where is Anne?
   Close to her man.
   Brown head, gold head,
     In and out the buttercups.

164

The Charcoal-Burner

The charcoal-burner has tales to tell.
He lives in the Forest,
Alone in the Forest;
He sits in the Forest,
Alone in the Forest.
And the sun comes slanting between the trees,
And rabbits come up, and they give him good-
 morning,
And rabbits come up and say, "Beautiful morning" . . .
And the moon swings clear of the tall black trees,
And owls fly over and wish him good-night,
Quietly over to wish him good-night . . .

And he sits and thinks of the things they know,
He and the Forest, alone together –
The springs that come and the summers that go,
Autumn dew on bracken and heather,
The drip of the Forest beneath the snow . . .

165

All the things they have seen,
All the things they have heard:
An April sky swept clean and the song of a bird . . .

Oh, the charcoal-burner has tales to tell!
And he lives in the Forest and knows us well.

Us Two

Wherever I am, there's always Pooh,
There's always Pooh and Me.
Whatever I do, he wants to do,
"Where are you going today?" says Pooh:
"Well, that's very odd 'cos I was too.
Let's go together," says Pooh, says he.
"Let's go together," says Pooh.

"What's twice eleven?" I said to Pooh,
("Twice what?" said Pooh to Me.)
"I *think* it ought to be twenty-two."
"Just what I think myself," said Pooh.
"It wasn't an easy sum to do,
But that's what it is," said Pooh, said he.
"That's what it is," said Pooh.

"Let's look for dragons," I said to Pooh.
"Yes, let's," said Pooh to Me.
We crossed the river and found a few –
"Yes, those are dragons all right," said Pooh.
"As soon as I saw their beaks I knew.
That's what they are," said Pooh, said he.
"That's what they are," said Pooh.

"Let's frighten the dragons," I said to Pooh.
"That's right," said Pooh to Me.
"*I'm* not afraid," I said to Pooh,
And I held his paw and shouted "Shoo!
Silly old dragons!" – and off they flew.
"I wasn't afraid," said Pooh, said he,
"I'm *never* afraid with you."

So wherever I am, there's always Pooh,
There's always Pooh and Me.
"What would I do?" I said to Pooh,
"If it wasn't for you," and Pooh said: "True,
It isn't much fun for One, but Two
Can stick together," says Pooh, says he.
"That's how it is," says Pooh.

The Old Sailor

There was once an old sailor my grandfather knew
Who had so many things which he wanted to do
That, whenever he thought it was time to begin,
He couldn't because of the state he was in.

He was shipwrecked, and lived on an island for weeks,

And he wanted a hat,

and he wanted some breeks;

And he wanted some nets, or a line and some hooks
For the turtles and things which you read of in books.

And, thinking of this, he remembered a thing
Which he wanted (for water) and that was a spring;
And he thought that to talk to he'd look for, and keep
(If he found it) a goat, or some chickens and sheep.

Then, because of the weather, he wanted a hut
With a door (to come in by) which opened and shut
(With a jerk, which was useful if snakes were about),
And a very strong lock to keep savages out.

He began on the fish-hooks, and when he'd begun
He decided he couldn't because of the sun.

So he knew what he ought to begin with, and that
Was to find, or to make, a large sun-stopping hat.

He was making the hat with some leaves from a tree,
When he thought, "I'm as hot as a body can be,
And I've nothing to take for my terrible thirst;
So I'll look for a spring, and I'll look for it *first*."

Then he thought as he started, "Oh, dear and oh, dear!
I'll be lonely to-morrow with nobody here!"
So he made in his note-book a couple of notes:
"*I must first find some chickens*"

174

and "*No, I mean goats.*"

He had just seen a goat (which he knew by the shape)
When he thought, "But I must have a boat for escape.
But a boat means a sail, which means needles and thread;
So I'd better sit down and make needles instead."

He began on a needle, but thought as he worked,
That, if this was an island where savages lurked,
Sitting safe in his hut he'd have nothing to fear,
Whereas now they might suddenly breathe in this ear!

So he thought of his hut . . . and he thought of his boat,
And his hat and his breeks, and his chickens and goat,
And the hooks (for his food) and the spring (for his
    thirst) . . .
But he *never* could think which he ought to do first.

176

And so in the end he did nothing at all,
But basked on the shingle wrapped up in a shawl.
And I think it was dreadful the way he behaved –
He did nothing but basking until he was saved!

The Engineer

Let it rain!
Who cares?
I've a train
Upstairs,
With a brake
Which I make
From a string
Sort of thing,
Which works
In jerks,
'Cos it drops
In the spring,
Which stops
With the string,

TIKITS

And the wheels
All stick
So quick
That it feels
Like a thing
That you make
With a brake,
Not string. . . .

So that's what I make,
When the day's all wet.
It's a good sort of brake
But it hasn't worked yet.

179

Journey's End

Christopher, Christopher, where are you going,
Christopher Robin?
 "Just up to the top of the hill,
 Upping and upping until
 I am right on the top of the hill,"
    Said Christopher Robin.

Christopher, Christopher, why are you going,
        Christopher Robin?
There's nothing to see, so when
You've got to the top, what then?
  "Just down to the bottom again,"
        Said Christopher Robin.

Furry Bear

If I were a bear,
   And a big bear too,
I shouldn't much care
   If it froze or snew;
I shouldn't much mind
   If it snowed or friz –
I'd be all fur-lined
   With a coat like his!

For I'd have fur boots and a brown fur wrap,
And brown fur knickers and a big fur cap.
I'd have a fur muffle-ruff to cover my jaws,
And brown fur mittens on my big brown paws.
With a big brown furry-down up to my head,
I'd sleep all the winter in a big fur bed.

Forgiven

I found a little beetle, so that Beetle was his name,
And I called him Alexander and he answered just the
    same.
I put him in a match-box, and I kept him all the
    day . . .
And Nanny let my beetle out –

Yes, Nanny let my beetle out –

She went and let my beetle out –

And Beetle ran away.

184

She said she didn't mean it,
and I never said she did,
She said she wanted matches
and she just took off the lid,

She said that she was sorry, but it's difficult to catch
An excited sort of beetle you've mistaken for a match.

She said that she was sorry, and I really mustn't mind,
As there's lots and lots of beetles which she's certain
we could find,
If we looked about the garden for the holes where
beetles hid –
And we'd get another match-box and write BEETLE
on the lid.

We went to all the places which a beetle might be near,
And we made the sort of noises which a beetle likes to hear,
And I saw a kind of something, and I gave a sort of shout:
"A beetle-house and Alexander Beetle coming out!"

185

It was Alexander Beetle I'm as certain as can be,
And he had a sort of look as if he thought it must
    be Me,

And he had a sort of look as if he thought he ought to say:
"I'm very very sorry that I tried to run away."

And Nanny's very sorry too for you-know-what-she-did,
And she's writing ALEXANDER very blackly on the lid,
So Nan and Me are friends, because it's difficult to catch
An excited Alexander you've mistaken for a match.

The Emperor's Rhyme

The King of Peru
(Who was Emperor too)
   Had a sort of a rhyme
    Which was useful to know,
If he felt very shy
When a stranger came by,
   Or they asked him the time
    When his watch didn't go;
Or supposing he fell
(By mistake) down a well,
   Or he tumbled when skating
    And sat on his hat,
Or perhaps wasn't told,
Till his porridge was cold –
   That his breakfast was waiting –
    Or something like that;

187

Oh, whenever the Emperor
Got into a temper, or
    Felt himself sulky or sad,
He would murmur and murmur,
Until he felt firmer,
    This curious rhyme which he had:

Eight eights are sixty-four,
    Multiply by seven.
When it's done,
Carry one
    And take away eleven.
Nine nines are eighty-one
    Multiply by three.
If it's more,
Carry four,
    And then it's time for tea.

188

So whenever the Queen
Took his armour to clean,
    And she didn't remember
        To use any starch;
Or his birthday (in May)
Was a horrible day,
    Being wet as November
        And windy as March;
Or, if sitting in state
With the Wise and the Great,
    He just happened to hiccup
        While signing his name,
Or the Queen gave a cough,
When his crown tumbled off
    As he bent down to pick up
        A pen for the same;

Oh, whenever the Emperor
Got into a temper, or
    Felt himself awkward and shy,

He would whisper and whisper,
Until he felt crisper,
   This odd little rhyme to the sky:

Eight eights are eighty-one;
   Multiply by seven.
If it's more,
Carry four,
   And take away eleven.
Nine nines are sixty-four;
   Multiply by three.
When it's done,
Carry one,
   And then it's time for tea.

190

Knight-in-armour

Whenever I'm a shining Knight,
I buckle on my armour tight;
And then I look about for things,
Like Rushings-out, and Rescuings,
And Savings from the Dragon's Lair,
And fighting all the Dragons there.
And sometimes when our fights begin,
I think I'll let the Dragons win . . .
And then I think perhaps I won't,
Because they're Dragons, and I don't.

Come Out With Me

There's sun on the river and sun on the hill . . .
You can hear the sea if you stand quite still!
There's eight new puppies at Roundabout Farm –
And I saw an old sailor with only one arm!

But every one says, "Run along!"
    (Run along, run along!)
All of them say, "Run along! I'm busy as can be."
    Every one says, "Run along,
    There's a little darling!"
If I'm a little darling, why don't they run with me?

There's wind on the river and wind on the hill . . .
There's a dark dead water-wheel under the mill!
I saw a fly which had just been drowned –
And I know where a rabbit goes into the ground!

But every one says, "Run along!"
    (Run along, run along!)
All of them say, "Yes, dear," and never notice me.
    Every one says, "Run along,
    There's a little darling!"
If I'm a little darling, why won't they come and see?

Down by the Pond

I'm fishing.
Don't talk, anybody, don't come near!
Can't you see that the fish might hear?
He thinks I'm playing with a piece of string;
He thinks I'm another sort of funny sort of thing.
    But he doesn't know I'm fishing –
    He doesn't know I'm fishing.
      That's what I'm doing –
        Fishing.

No, I'm not, I'm newting.
Don't cough, anybody, don't come by!
Any small noise makes a newt feel shy.
He thinks I'm a bush, or a new sort of tree;
He thinks it's somebody, but doesn't think it's Me.
    And he doesn't know I'm newting –
    No, he doesn't know I'm newting.
      That's what I'm doing –
        Newting.

The Little Black Hen

Berryman and Baxter,
  Prettiboy and Penn
And old Farmer Middleton
  Are five big men . . .
And all of them were after.
  The Little Black Hen.

She ran quickly,
  They ran fast;

196

Baxter was first, and
　Berryman was last.
I sat and watched
　By the old plum-tree . . .
She squawked through the hedge
　And she came to me.

The Little Black Hen
　Said, "Oh, it's you!"
I said, "Thank you,
　How do you do?
And please will you tell me,
　Little Black Hen,
What did they want,
　Those five big men?"

197

The Little Black Hen
   She said to me:
"They want me to lay them
   An egg for tea.
If they were Emperors,
   If they were Kings,
I'm much too busy
   To lay them things."

"I'm not a King
   And I haven't a crown:
I climb up trees,
   And I tumble down.
I can shut one eye,
   I can count to ten,
So lay me and egg, please,
   Little Black Hen."

The Little Black Hen said,
   "What will you pay,

198

If I lay you an egg
  For Easter Day?"

"I'll give you a Please
  And a How-do-you-do,
I'll show you a Bear
  Who lives in the Zoo,
I'll show you the nettle-place
  On my leg,
If you'll lay me a great big
  Eastery egg."

The Little Black Hen
  Said, "I don't care
For a How-do-you-do
  Or a Big-brown-bear,
But I'll lay you a beautiful
  Eastery egg,
If you'll show me the nettle-place
  On your leg."

I showed her the place
  Where I had my sting.
She touched it gently
  With one black wing.
"Nettles don't hurt

If you count to ten.
And now for the egg,"
    Said the Little Black Hen.

When I wake up
    On Easter Day,
I shall see my egg
    She's promised to lay.
If I were Emperors,
    If I were Kings,
It couldn't be fuller
    Of wonderful things.

Berryman and Baxter,
Prettiboy and Penn,
And old Farmer Middleton
Are five big men.
All of them are wanting
An egg for their tea,
But the Little Black Hen is much too busy,
The Little Black Hen is *much* too busy,
The Little Black Hen is MUCH too busy . . .
She's laying my egg for me!

The Friend

There are lots and lots of people who are always asking
    things,
Like Dates and Pounds-and-ounces and the names of
    funny Kings,
And the answer's either Sixpence or A Hundred Inches
    Long.
And I know they'll think me silly if I get the answer wrong.

So Pooh and I go whispering, and Pooh looks very bright,
And says, "Well, *I* say sixpence, but I don't suppose I'm
    right."
And then it doesn't matter what the answer ought to be,
'Cos if he's right, I'm Right, and if he's wrong, it isn't Me.

The Good Little Girl

It's funny how often they say to me, "Jane?
  "Have you been a *good* girl?"
  "Have you been a *good* girl?"
And when they have said it, they say it again,
  "Have you been a *good* girl?"
  "Have you been a *good* girl?"

I go to a party, I go out to tea,
I go to an aunt for a week at the sea,
I come back from school or from playing a game;
Wherever I come from, it's always the same;
  "Well?
Have you been a *good* girl, Jane?"

203

204

It's always the end of the loveliest day:
  "Have you been a *good* girl?"
  "Have you been a *good* girl?"
I went to the Zoo, and they waited to say:
  "Have you been a *good* girl?"
  "Have you been a *good* girl?"

Well, what did they think that I went there to do?
And why should I want to be bad at the Zoo?
And should I be likely to say if I had?
So that's why it's funny of Mummy and Dad,
This asking and asking, in case I was bad,
  "Well?
  Have you been a *good* girl, Jane?"

205

A Thought

If I were John and John were Me,
Then he'd be six and I'd be three.
If John were Me and I were John,
I shouldn't have these trousers on.

King Hilary and the Beggarman

Of Hilary the Great and Good
    They tell a tale at Christmas time.
I've often thought the story would
Be prettier but just as good
If almost anybody should
    Translate it into rime.
So I have done the best I can
For lack of some more learned man.

Good King Hilary
Said to his Chancellor
(Proud Lord Willoughby,
Lord High Chancellor):
"Run to the wicket-gate
Quickly, quickly,
Run to the wicket-gate
    And see who is knocking.
It may be a rich man,
Sea-borne from Araby,
Bringing me peacocks,
Emeralds and ivory;
It may be a poor man,
Travel-worn and weary,
Bringing me oranges
    To put in my stocking."

Proud Lord Willoughby,
Lord High Chancellor,
    Laughed both loud and free:*
"I've served Your Majesty, man to man,
Since first Your Majesty's reign began,
And I've often walked, but I never, never ran,
    Never, never, never," quoth he.

Good King Hilary
Said to his Chancellor
(Proud Lord Willoughby,
Lord High Councellor):

*Haw! Haw! Haw!

208

"Walk to the wicket-gate
Quickly, quickly,
Walk to the wicket-gate
    And see who is knocking.
It may be a captain,
Hawk-nosed, bearded,
Bringing me gold-dust,
Spices, and sandalwood;

It may be a scullion,
Care-free, whistling,
Bringing me sugar-plums
    To put in my stocking."

Proud Lord Willoughby,
Lord High Chancellor,
    Laughed both loud and free:
"I've served in the Palace since I was four,
And I'll serve in the Palace a-many years more,
And I've opened a window, but never a door,
    Never, never, never," quoth he.

Good King Hilary
Said to his Chancellor
(Proud Lord Willoughby,
Lord High Chancellor):
"Open the window
Quickly, quickly,
Open the window
    And see who is knocking.

It may be a waiting-maid,
Apple-cheeked, dimpled,
Sent by her mistress
To bring me greeting;

210

It may be children,
Anxious, whispering,
Bringing me cobnuts,
    To put in my stocking."

Proud Lord Willoughby,
Lord High Chancellor,
    Laughed both loud and free:
"I'll serve Your Majesty till I die –
As Lord Chancellor, not as spy
To peep from lattices; no, not I,
    Never, never, never," quoth he.

Good King Hilary
Looked at his Chancellor
(Proud Lord Willoughby,
Lord High Chancellor):

He said no word
To his stiff-set Chancellor,
But ran to the wicket-gate
   To see who was knocking.
He found no rich man
Trading from Araby;
He found no captain,
Blue-eyed, weather-tanned;
He found no waiting-maid
Sent by her mistress;
But only a beggarman
   With one red stocking.

Good King Hilary
Looked at the beggarman,
   And laughed him three times three;
And he turned that beggarman round about:
"Your thews are strong, and your arm is stout;
Come, throw me a Lord High Chancellor out,
   And take his place," quoth he.

Of Hilary the Good and Great
Old wives at Christmas time relate
This tale, which points, at any rate,
   Two morals on the way.

The first: "*Whatever Fortune brings,*
Don't be afraid of doing things."
(Especially, of course, for Kings.)
     It also seems to say
(But not so wisely): "*He who begs*
With one red stocking on his legs
Will be, as sure as eggs are eggs,
     A Chancellor some day."

Swing Song

Here I go up in my swing
    Ever so high.
I am the King of the fields, and the King
    Of the town.
I am the King of the earth, and the King
    Of the sky.
Here I go up in my swing . . .
    Now I go down.

Explained

Elizabeth Ann
Said to her Nan:
"Please will you tell me how God began?
Somebody must have made Him. So
Who could it be, 'cos I want to know?"
And Nurse said, "*Well!*"
And Ann said, "Well?
I know you know, and I wish you'd tell."
And Nurse took pins from her mouth, and said,
"Now then, darling, it's time for bed."

Elizabeth Ann
Had a wonderful plan:
She would run round the world till she found a man
Who knew *exactly* how God began.

216

She got up early, she dressed, and ran
Trying to find an Important Man.
She ran to London and knocked at the door
Of the Lord High Doodelum's coach-and-four.
"Please, sir (if there's anyone in),
However-and-ever did God begin?"

The Lord High Doodelum lay in bed,
But out of the window, large and red,
Came the Lord High Coachman's face instead.
And the Lord High Coachman's laughed and said:
"Well, what put *that* in your quaint little head?"

Elizabeth Ann went home again
And took from the ottoman Jennifer Jane.
"Jenniferjane," said Elizabeth Ann,
"Tell me *at once* how God began."
And Jane, who didn't much care for speaking,
Replied in her usual way by squeaking.

What did it mean? Well, to be quite candid,
I don't know, but Elizabeth Ann did.
Elizabeth Ann said softly, "Oh!
Thank you, Jennifer. Now I know."

218

Twice Times

There were Two little Bears who lived in a Wood,
And one of them was Bad and the other was Good.
Good Bear learnt his Twice Times One –
But Bad Bear left all his buttons undone.

They lived in a Tree when the weather was hot,
And one of them was Good, and the other was Not.
Good Bear learnt his Twice Times Two –
But Bad Bear's thingummies were worn right through.

219

They lived in a Cave when the weather was cold,
And they Did, and they Didn't Do, what they were
    told.
Good Bear learnt his Twice Times Three –
But Bad Bear *never* had his hand-ker-chee.

They lived in the Wood with a Kind Old Aunt,
And one said "*Yes'm,*" and the other said "*Shan't!*"
Good Bear learnt his Twice Times Four –
But Bad Bear's knicketies were terrible tore.

220

And then quite suddenly (just like Us)
One got Better and the other got Wuss.
Good Bear muddled his Twice Times Three –
But Bad Bear coughed *in his hand-ker-chee*!

Good Bear muddled his Twice Times Two –
But Bad Bear's thingummies looked like new.
Good Bear muddled his Twice Times One –
But Bad Bear *never* left his buttons undone.

221

There may be a Moral, though some say not;
I think there's a moral, though I don't know what.
But if one gets better, as the other gets wuss,
These Two Little Bears are just like Us.
For Christopher remembers up to Twice Times Ten . . .
But *I* keep forgetting where I've put my pen.*

* *So I have had to write this one in pencil.*

The Morning Walk

When Anne and I go out for a walk,
We hold each other's hand and talk
Of all the things we mean to do
When Anne and I are forty-two.

And when we've thought about a thing,
Like bowling hoops or bicycling,
Or falling down on Anne's balloon,
We do it in the afternoon.

Cradle Song

O Timothy Tim
  Has ten pink toes,
  And ten pink toes
Has Timothy Tim.
They go with him
  Wherever he goes,
  And wherever he goes
They go with him.

O Timothy Tim
  Has two blue eyes,
  And two blue eyes
Has Timothy Tim.
They cry with him
  Whenever he cries,
  And whenever he cries,
They cry with him.

226

O Timothy Tim
  Has one red head,
  And one red head
Has Timothy Tim.
It sleeps with him
  In Timothy's bed.
  Sleep well, red head
Of Timothy Tim.

Waiting at the Window

These are my two drops of rain
Waiting on the window-pane.

I am waiting here to see
Which the winning one will be.

Both of them have different names.
One is John and one is James.

All the best and all the worst
Comes from which of them is first.

James has just begun to ooze.
He's the one I want to lose.

John is waiting to begin.
He's the one I want to win.

James is going slowly on.
Something sort of sticks to John.

John is moving off at last.
James is going pretty fast.

John is rushing down the pane.
James is going slow again.

James has met a sort of smear.
John is getting very near.

Is he going fast enough?
(James has found a piece of fluff.)

John has hurried quickly by.
(James was talking to a fly.)

John is there, and John has won!
Look! I told you! Here's the sun!

Pinkle Purr

Tattoo was the mother of Pinkle Purr,
A little black nothing of feet and fur;
And by-and-by, when his eyes came through,
He saw his mother, the big Tattoo.
And all that he learned he learned from her.
"I'll ask my mother," says Pinkle Purr.

Tattoo was the mother of Pinkle Purr,
A ridiculous kitten with silky fur.
And little black Pinkle grew and grew
Till he got as big as the big Tattoo.
And all that he did he did with her.
"Two friends together," says Pinkle Purr.

Tattoo was the mother of Pinkle Purr,
An adventurous cat in a coat of fur.
And whenever he thought of a thing to do,
He didn't much bother about Tattoo,
For he knows it's nothing to do with her,
So "See you later," says Pinkle Purr.

Tattoo is the mother of Pinkle Purr,
An enormous leopard with coal-black fur.
A little brown kitten that's nearly new
Is now playing games with its big Tattoo . . .
And Pink looks lazily down at her:
"Dear little Tat," says Pinkle Purr.

Wind on the Hill

No one can tell me,
   Nobody knows,
Where the wind comes from,
   Where the wind goes.

It's flying from somewhere
    As fast as it can,
I couldn't keep up with it,
    Not if I ran.

But if I stopped holding
    The string of my kite,
It would blow with the wind
    For a day and a night.

And then when I found it,
    Wherever it blew,
I should know that the wind
    Had been going there too.

So then I could tell them
    Where the wind goes . . .
But where the wind comes from
    Nobody knows.

Forgotten

Lords of the Nursery
  Wait in a row,
Five on the high wall,
  And four on the low;
Big Kings and Little Kings,
  Brown Bears and Black,
All of them waiting
  Till John comes back.

Some think that John boy
  Is lost in the wood,
Some say he couldn't be,
  Some say he could.

235

Some think that John boy
    Hides on the hill;
Some say he won't come back,
    Some say he will.

High was the sun, when
    John went away . . .
Here they've been waiting
    All through the day;
Big Bears and Little Bears,
    White Kings and Black,
All of them waiting
    Till John comes back.

Lords of the Nursery
    Looked down the hill,
Some saw the sheep-fold,
    Some saw the mill;

Some saw the roofs
  Of the little grey town . . .
And their shadows grew long
  As the sun slipt down.

Gold between the poplars
  An old moon shows;
Silver up the star-way
  The full moon rose;
Silver down the star-way
  The old moon crept . . .
And, one by another,
  The grey fields slept.

Lords of the Nursery
  Their still watch keep . . .
They hear from the sheep-fold
  The rustle of sheep.

A young bird twitters
  And hides its head;
A little wind suddenly
  Breathes, and is dead.

Slowly and slowly
  Dawns the new day . . .
What's become of John boy?

No one can say.
Some think that John boy
  Is lost on the hill;
Some say he won't come back,
  Some say he will.

What's become of John boy?
Nothing at all,
He played with his skipping rope,
He played with his ball.
He ran after butterflies,
Blue ones and red;
He did a hundred happy things –
And then went to bed.

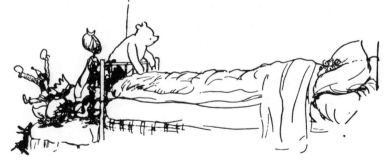

In the Dark

I've had my supper,
    And *had* my supper,
        And HAD my supper and all;
I've heard the story
    Of Cinderella,
        And how she went to the ball;
I've cleaned my teeth,
    And I've said my prayers,
        And I've cleaned and said them right;
And they've all of them been
    And kissed me lots,
        They've all of them said, "Good-night."

So – here I am in the dark alone,
    There's nobody here to see;

I think to myself,
I play to myself,
And nobody knows what I say to myself;
Here I am in the dark alone,
What is it going to be?
I can think whatever I like to think,
I can play whatever I like to play,
I can laugh whatever I like to laugh,
There's nobody here but me.

I'm talking to a rabbit . . .
I'm talking to the sun . . .
I think I am a hundred –
I'm one.

241

I'm lying in a forest . . .
   I'm lying in a cave . . .
I'm talking to a Dragon . . .
   I'm BRAVE.
I'm lying on my left side . . .
   I'm lying on my right . . .
I'll play a lot tomorrow . . .

    . . . .

I'll think a lot tomorrow . . .

    . . . .

I'll laugh . . .
    a lot . . .
       tomorrow . . .
      (Heigh-ho!)
          Good-night.

The End

When I was One,
I had just begun.

When I was Two,
I was nearly new.

When I was Three,
I was hardly Me.

When I was Four,
I was not much more.

When I was Five,
I was just alive.

But now I am Six, I'm as clever as clever.
So I think I'll be six now for ever and ever.